DINOSAURS!

A Spot-the-Difference Puzzle Book

By **Steve Parker**   Illustrated by **Charles Fuge**

Random House New York

Introduction

Could anyone ever have imagined a group of animals as wonderful and diverse as the dinosaurs? For 150 million years these mighty animals ruled the earth, from *Diplodocus*, a 90-foot plant-eater, to *Compsognathus*, a swift hunter no bigger than a cat.

On the following pages you will find vivid and colorful scenes from the Age of Dinosaurs. They show how the dinosaurs fought to survive, until finally some kind of worldwide disaster brought their long reign to a sudden end.

At first, the pictures on the facing pages may seem identical. But look again. There are ten differences for you to find between each pair – an *Ichthyosaurus* gives birth to her baby, the hunter *Deinonychus* reveals its terrible slashing claw, and one of the first mammals appears, cautiously observing the giant reptiles that share its world. All of these and more are here for you to discover in ten challenging picture puzzles.

How to use this book

Look at the pictures and imagine yourself in a strange and unfamiliar world. Try to spot all ten changes between each pair of pictures. If you get stuck, you will find a key to the changes on the pages that follow, plus lots of fascinating information about the amazing creatures that once roamed the world.

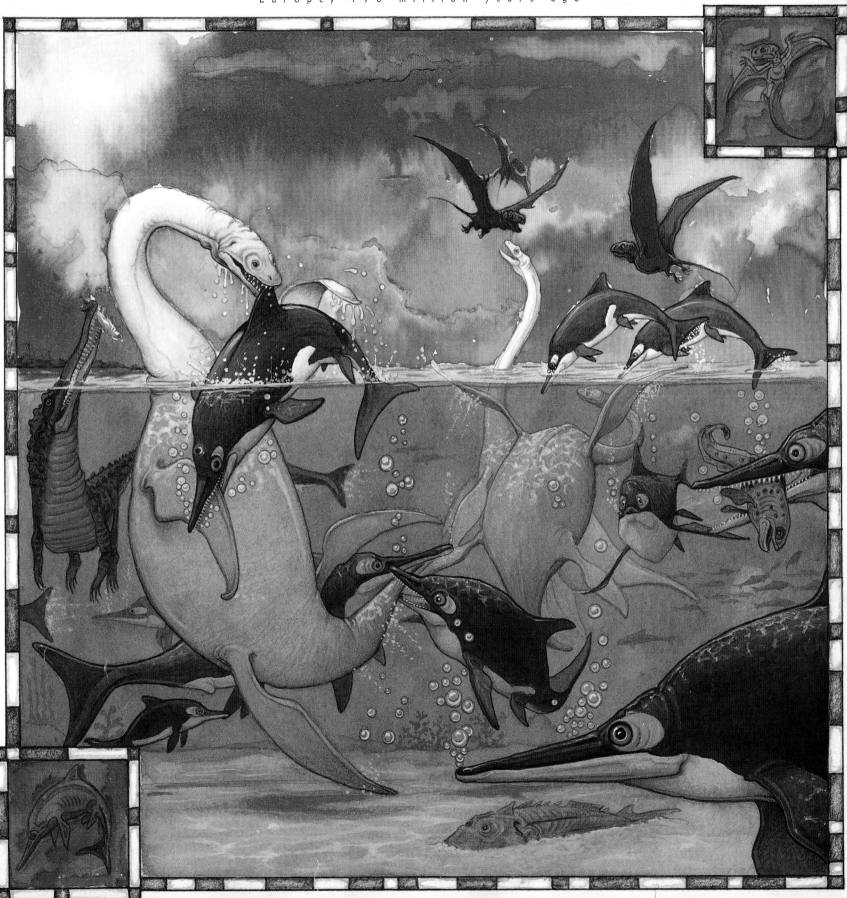

TIME: The Early Jurassic Period, 190 million years ago

PLACE: The warm, shallow seas that once covered parts of Europe

REPTILES: *Ichthyosaurus*, the best-known of the ichthyosaurs; *Plesiosaurus*, one of the first plesiosaurs; *Teleosaurus*, a sea-dwelling member of the crocodile group; and *Dimorphodon*, a pterosaur

Battle at Sea

The Age of Dinosaurs began about 220 million years ago. By the start of the Jurassic Period, 213 million years ago, many dinosaurs roamed the land, and the waters teemed with reptiles such as ichthyosaurs ("fish-lizards"), plesiosaurs and pliosaurs, with their paddle limbs, all superbly adapted to (able to survive in) the aquatic environment. This group of ichthyosaurs is attacking a larger but slower plesiosaur, which darts out its long neck and snaps back at its tormentors. The plesiosaur is not their usual prey. Ichthyosaurs had dolphin-shaped bodies and probably hunted in the same way as modern dolphins, by pursuing swift-swimming fish and squid.

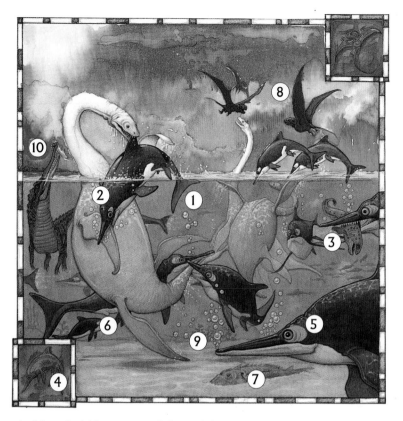

1. More bubbles appear. Most of the animals shown here were reptiles, which means they had lungs and breathed air. They would come to the surface regularly, to expel the stale air from their lungs and breathe in fresh air. Occasionally small bubbles might escape from their mouths while they were under water. (The exceptions are the fish, which breathed using gills.)

2. *Ichthyosaurus* has a blowhole. These holes were the creature's main breathing openings. To breathe, *Ichthyosaurus* had to break the water with only its face. During evolution, the nostrils moved from the usual reptile position near the tip of the snout to the rear near the eyes. The nostrils, or "blowholes," of dolphins and whales have moved even further during their evolution and are on top of the foreheads. So these animals must break the water with even less of their bodies than the ichthyosaurs did.

3. *Ichthyosaurus*' rear paddle moves. The ancestor of this reptile once lived on land, but as it adapted to the water, its limbs evolved into oar-like paddles. The original leg bones, including the toes, were still inside the paddle but all traces of the thigh, knee, hip, and ankle were lost.

4. The backbone of *Ichthyosaurus* angles down into the tail. The individual vertebrae, or bones of the spinal column, bent down into the lower tail lobe. The muscles along each side of the backbone contracted in turn to swish the tail from side to side, and so propeled *Ichthyosaurus* through the ocean. In addition, *Ichthyosaurus* fossils (fossils are the hardened remains of dead plants and animals) found in Germany still have the faint impressions of the skin and flesh around the bones, so we are sure this creature had a two-part tail and a dorsal (back) fin.

5. *Ichthyosaurus* has regained its eye markings. We have no clear clues about the color or patterning of this reptile's skin. Perhaps it was marked like a killer whale, with a black upper side and a white belly. As with killer whales, the precise pattern might vary from one individual to another, so that the ichthyosaurs could recognize one another. It is even possible that they could change color, like modern cuttlefish or chameleons.

6. A mother *Ichthyosaurus* has given birth to her baby. Some of the amazingly detailed ichthyosaur fossils show the bones of small specimens, presumably babies, within the bodies of an adult, presumably a mother. A few specimens seem to show the babies emerging from the mother's body – tail-first, the way dolphins and whales are born. *Ichthyosaurus* could not walk onto land to lay its eggs, so it gave birth in the water.

7. The fish is more deeply buried in the sand. *Ichthyosaurus* was about 6 1/2 feet (2 meters) in length. Other ichthyosaurs grew much larger, with some more than 23 feet (7 meters) long. All members of the group were streamlined predators, with rows of small, sharp teeth. They would present a threat to almost any ocean dweller – even a large fish like this one.

8. *Dimorphodon* loses its tiny wing-claws. In all pterosaurs (flying reptiles), the thin, light, elastic membrane of each wing was supported along the front by the immensely elongated bones of the fourth finger. The first three fingers formed small claws, for gripping, hanging, or walking. *Dimorphodon* had a wingspan of about 4 feet (1.2 meters).

9. There is more seaweed. Seaweeds, or algae, were one of the earliest plants to appear. In ancient times, as today, they were the basis of food chains in the ocean. These plants fed small animals, which were eaten by bigger ones, and so on. Some algae were large, like those shown here. Others were microscopic and drifted in the surface waters, forming prehistoric plankton.

10. A tropical island appears in the distance behind *Teleosaurus*. Through the ages, continents have slowly drifted around the globe, and islands have appeared and disappeared, though perhaps not quite this fast! Some islands were formed when underwater volcanoes erupted and built up red-hot, steaming layers of rock. Others formed from coral reefs, made from the stony, cup-shaped skeletons of billions of tiny jelly-bodied creatures called coral polyps.

TIME: The Late Jurassic Period, 150 million years ago

PLACE: Midwestern North America (now Dakota-Wyoming)

DINOSAURS: *Allosaurus*, a large and fearsome predator; *Ornitholestes*, a smaller, lighter hunter; *Iguanodon*, a fairly big, two-legged plant-eater; *Apatosaurus*, a sauropod (huge, long-necked herbivore); *Brachylophosaurus*, a Cretaceous hadrosaur

The Crowded Waterhole

Life depends on water. In anywhere but the swampiest landscape, the rivers, lakes and other watering places are magnets for wildlife. The moisture encourages plant growth, which attracts herbivorous (plant-eating) animals, which in turn draw the carnivores (meat-eaters). A waterhole is also a meeting of two very different habitats – terrestrial (land) and aquatic (water). Floating water plants provide cover for fish and other aquatic animals, which are keenly watched by land-based predators on the bank. Amphibious creatures, from frogs to crocodiles, are at home in either habitat.

1. *Allosaurus* looks forward to a mouth-watering meal. Reptiles have salivary glands in each side of their heads, which make the watery substance saliva (spit). This helps the animal lubricate and swallow its bite-size lumps of food. Dinosaurs probably drooled, too. In a few seconds, *Allosaurus* will rush its 32-foot (10-meter), 2-ton bulk from hiding, and charge its selected victim.

2. *Ornitholestes* appears on the lakeshore. Another carnivore drawn by the presence of herbivores, this nimble hunter had a head and body about the size of a greyhound dog. Its tail was as long as its head and body put together. Each large hand had three long, strong fingers tipped with sharp, cruel-looking claws. The hands were ideal for gripping small prey such as lizards, mammals, insects, and baby dinosaurs.

3. *Iguanodon* no longer has its large thumb-spike. Possibly its only means of defense, *Iguanodon's* sharp thumb was like a slim, strong dagger of bone. It could be jabbed into the eye or neck of an attacker such as *Allosaurus*. This 29-foot (9-meter) plant-eater,

which weighed 4 tons, is one of the best-known of all dinosaurs and was one of the most widespread. Hundreds of fossil skeletons have been found in Europe and North America.

4. *Brachylophosaurus* has grown a crest and changed into *Tsintaosaurus*. These two dinosaurs were both hadrosaurs ("duck-billed dinosaurs") and lived at the end of the Cretaceous Period (75 million years ago). *Brachylophosaurus* ("short-crested reptile") lacked the distinctive hadrosaur crest. Instead, it had a thickened roof to its skull, like a bony crash helmet. Perhaps it had head-to-head pushing or butting contests, to win mates or gain dominance in the herd. Some experts believe that *Tsintaosaurus* had a tube-like crest sticking up from its head. Others believe that *Tsintaosaurus* wasn't a real dinosaur at all but a mix of fossils from several animals.

5. *Apatosaurus* changes color. We can only guess what color the dinosaurs were. This enormous herbivore may have had different colors to identify the sexes for breeding and to mark out the group leaders. Some of today's reptiles, like chameleons, can change their color for camouflage. But *Apatosaurus* was 65 feet (20 meters) in length, with a body as big as a tractor-trailer. Camouflage was unlikely to help!

6. An *Apatosaurus* leans on a tree to knock it down. To bring the topmost leaves within reach of its small, peg-shaped teeth, this 25-ton mound of flesh and bone would uproot the entire tree. Because of a naming mix-up, this sauropod was once called *Brontosaurus* ("thunder reptile"). Its correct name is now *Apatosaurus* ("deceptive reptile"). Officially, there is now no dinosaur called *Brontosaurus*.

7. A fish cruises close to the surface. To a carnivore, the edible attractions of the water included fish, frogs and other amphibians, freshwater shellfish, and various worms and aquatic insects. *Ornitholestes* may have scooped up fish with its long fingers, although getting that close to the water would have put it in danger – a fellow reptile, the large crocodile *Protosuchus*, lurks nearby.

8. The handprint changes to a footprint. Fossilized footprints give many clues about the animals who made them. The clues include the basic foot size; the weight of the maker; and the stride, or distance between footprints, which shows how fast the maker walked or ran. Many footprints of the same kind, close to each other, suggest a pack or herd on the move, or one animal following a regular route.

9. A pterosaur has grown a tail. There were two main groups of pterosaurs (see page 41). First came the rhamphorhynchoids, which possessed long, bony tails. They all became extinct (died out) at the end of the Jurassic Period. Just before this, the second group, the pterodactyloids, appeared. They lacked a tail, but had a long, bony crest on the back of the head. Perhaps this replaced the tail's stabilizing and steering jobs in flight. These pterosaurs are *Rhamphorhynchus*, with a wingspan of about 5 feet (1.5 meters).

10. The water plants have changed color. Water lilies were among the first flowering plants to evolve in the Early Cretaceous Period (see page 37). Putting them in this Late Jurassic scene may be stretching a point, but recent fossil evidence has been pushing back the appearance of flowering plants, placing them ever earlier than previously believed.

TIME: The Late Jurassic Period, 150 million years ago

PLACE: Central Europe (now Bavaria, Germany)

DINOSAURS: *Compsognathus*, one of the smallest dinosaurs; *Coelurus*, a two-legged coelurosaur 6 1/2 feet (2 meters) long (both were agile meat-eaters)

In the Undergrowth

Most dinosaur re-creations in museums make us look up at huge, long-necked beasts striding across open countryside, or great fearsome-fanged meat-eaters battling with tanklike victims. However, there were also plenty of mini-dinos, who spent their days skulking among the thick ferns and palm-like cycads of the Jurassic undergrowth. They were important links in the food chains, preying on insects and other little creatures, and scavenging what they could from bigger carcasses. *Compsognathus* was hardly larger than a pet cat, with a head as big as a human hand. *Coelurus* was only twice this size.

1. ***Coelurus'* tail is straight.** The fossil bones from the tails of these dinosaurs indicate that the joints between them were fairly bendable, giving the whole tail whip-like flexibility. This would help the dinosaur when it ran on its two legs, since it could adjust the tail to counterbalance its body. The tail could also be swung to the side, to help turn corners at high speeds.

2. ***Coelurus'* tongue lolls from its mouth.** Yes, dinosaurs had tongues, just like snakes, lizards, and other modern reptiles. At least, that's what we assume. Tongues are almost solid muscle and do not fossilize, but the supporting neck bones that have been found indicate that dinosaurs did have tongues. The color is guesswork, but why not blue? Today's blue-tongued skink, an aptly named lizard from Australia, has an extremely vivid tongue!

3. ***Coelurus* has scars on its flanks.** These little dinosaurs would have been potential meals for the big hunters – carnosaurs such as *Allosaurus*. However, their small size, slim shape, and agility could all combine to help them wriggle free from the jaws and

claws of the predator. In many cases, the victims would escape with their lives but be left with flesh wounds. These wounds would heal in time and leave a lumpy scar on the dinosaur's scaly skin.

4. *Coelurus'* ear is rounded, not slit-like. Dinosaurs had ears, like reptiles today, but they would have come in many different shapes and sizes. The eardrum was simply a thin, taut area of skin on the side of the head, among the scales; there was no earflap, as in mammals. Fossilized versions of the long, rod-like bone that connected the eardrum to the sound-sensing organ deeper in the head, near the brain, have been discovered.

5. *Coelurus'* prey has changed from a reptile to a mammal. It's likely that early shrew-like mammals as well as small reptiles shared the undergrowth with the smaller dinosaurs, slipping quietly among the roots and shoots. Like lizards and snakes today, *Coelurus* and *Compsognathus* would have needed sharp senses and fast coordination to seize such alert, agile prey.

6. The passing butterfly has developed eye-like patterns on its wings. Many kinds of insects were well established by the Age of Dinosaurs, and new kinds were evolving all the time. Some preserved butterfly wings reveal patterns that include rounded shapes like eyes. The resting butterfly would startle an attacker by opening its wings suddenly to reveal what looked like the big-eyed face of a predator!

7. There are more feathers on the forest floor. During the Late Jurassic Period, feathers were one of evolution's newest inventions. Flying insects and pterosaurs were being joined in the air by the first birds, such as *Archaeopteryx* (see page 24). The feathers may have been discarded naturally as the bird molted (shed) them. Or they could be leftovers from *Coelurus'* last meal!

8. Extra water droplets have appeared on the leaves. The climate during this period was relatively warm and damp, with plenty of rainfall. In the undergrowth, shaded from the drying sun by the conifer trees above and sheltered from drying winds, the leaves would drip with raindrops for many hours after a shower.

9. Some of the mushrooms are different colors. The moist, shaded soil of the Jurassic forest floor provided ideal conditions for mushrooms, toadstools, and similar fungi. However, fungi rotted away or were quickly eaten; they were too soft to be preserved as fossils. So the fungal fossil record is extremely sparse. The origins of fungi, and the time of their first appearance, is a hotly debated topic.

10. The dinosaur fossil is now a preserved insect. This insect alighted on a conifer tree trunk, only to be trapped by sticky resin, or sap, oozing from the bark. Its feet got stuck. More resin flowed and covered its body. Over millions of years, the resin fossilized into the golden see-through substance we call amber, allowing us to view the entombed insect in all its intricate detail.

TIME: The Late Jurassic Period, 150 million years ago

PLACE: Midwestern North America

DINOSAUR: *Diplodocus*, one of the long-necked, long-tailed, barrel-bodied, plant-eating sauropod group

Journey Through the Snow

During the Jurassic Period, the world's climate was warmer and wetter than it is today. Even so, flurries of snow probably sprinkled the hilly northern areas during the cool season. This herd of *Diplodocus* is migrating (traveling) away from the hills, where they have been feeding on the summer growth of plants. These great sauropods would not survive winter in the uplands, so they migrate toward the milder, more sheltered valleys for the cool season. Every year, some of them perish on the way. Those that reach the valley will find enough vegetation to fuel their immense 10-ton bulks.

1. A snow shower signals the approach of winter. As the air temperature drops and sleet and snow begin to fall, the dinosaurs' bodies cool down. They begin to move more slowly. If the oncoming cold weather catches up with them, the freezing temperatures mean certain death. They must keep moving, in a race against the increasing cold.

2. A small plant has lost some of its leaves. Migrating animals have to balance the benefits of stopping to eat against taking longer on the journey and putting themselves in peril. *Diplodocus* has raked off the leaves of this plant. However, the plants can survive this natural pruning and will sprout new leaves when the warmth returns.

3. A hungry *Diplodocus* tries to munch on tree bark – but with little success. The mouth of *Diplodocus* was designed to swallow food whole. Its teeth were too small, blunt, and peg-like for tough, stringy bark. They were good for pulling off and raking in soft, leafy vegetation like the cycads. This dinosaur's biting and chewing muscles were weak, so tree bark was an unsuitable food, both in texture and nutritional value.

4. Branches have been stripped from a tree. The immensely long neck of *Diplodocus* was primarily a food-gathering device. Without moving a step, this dinosaur could sweep its head 32 feet (10 meters) in any direction, including straight up. A previous herd of *Diplodocus* had already stripped the branches, producing a well-defined "browse line" in the trees.

5. A *Diplodocus* head appears, scanning the undergrowth from its great height for predators and other dangers. *Diplodocus* holds the record as the longest of all dinosaurs that are known from complete skeletons. It measured 90 feet (27 meters) from nose tip to tail end. The long neck gave it a bird's-eye view over shrubs and low trees. But compared to other sauropods, *Diplodocus* was relatively slim and light, at only 10-15 tons.

6. A baby *Diplodocus* appears toward the rear of the group. In the yearly life cycle, the *Diplodocus* herd bred in the warm season, so that their babies hatched when there was plenty of plant food. The onset of colder weather slowed plant growth, which meant less food. It was a critical time for the year's recently hatched youngsters.

7. Some of the dinosaur carcass has been eaten by scavengers. Scavengers arrived almost at once to feed on the carcasses of dead animals. This dinosaur was probably old and at the end of its natural lifespan. We do not know how long dinosaurs lived. Judging by the growth rates of today's large reptiles, the sauropods could have reached over 100 years of age.

8. The forest has spread across the landscape. Flowering plants had probably not evolved yet, so there would be no flowers or blossom trees in the Jurassic landscape. But there were plenty of cycads and other palm-tree-like plants. Conifers, like firs, spruces, and pines, with their needle-like

evergreen leaves, formed great forests. Indeed, the Jurassic Period was the heyday of the conifer trees. Their numbers and range have been decreasing ever since, as broad-leaved trees, like oaks and maples, have taken over. Conifers are now found mostly in mountainous northern regions.

9. A cone opens to release its seeds. Cones are the reproductive parts of the conifer trees. Smaller male cones release tiny windblown pollen grains, which pollinate the larger female cones and begin seed development. When the seeds are ripe, the female cones open up and allow them to drift away, to settle and grow into new trees – or be eaten.

10. Another mammal appears, feeding on the dinosaur carcass. The first small, shrew-like mammals appeared only slightly after the first dinosaurs, over 200 million years ago. Their warm-blooded bodies and insulating fur enabled them to stay active through the cold season and at night, when they could avoid the attentions of the larger dinosaurs. All through the reign of the dinosaurs, the mammals continued to evolve slowly, with none growing larger than a pet cat.

TIME: The Late Jurassic Period, 150 million years ago

PLACE: Islands in a warm, shallow sea that covered what is now southern Germany

REPTILES: *Archaeopteryx*, the earliest known bird

A Bird's-Eye View

It's busy and noisy at the seaside. Colorful creatures run powerfully on two legs along the ground, crawl and clamber up the tree trunks, spread their wings to flap and flutter among the branches, then rest and comb their feathers, before snapping after insects. There's nothing odd about this, except that these are a brand-new kind of animal. They are the first birds the world has ever seen – *Archaeopteryx* ("ancient wing"). On the ground below, their very close relatives, the small coelurosaurs, chase after smaller creatures. Up in the branches, *Archaeopteryx* has a whole new habitat to explore and exploit for food, shelter, safety, and nesting sites.

1. More vines have grown. *Archaeopteryx* probably made use of the clawholds that vines gave to climb through the branches of trees. Any development that gave an edge over ground-based competitors would provide new possibilities for evolution. Why not take to life in the trees? And then to life in the air?

2. A dead *Archaeopteryx* floats on the water's surface. We owe our extensive knowledge of *Archaeopteryx* to its very detailed fossils, preserved in extremely fine-grained limestone. These fossils formed on the bed of an ancient shallow sea, probably when *Archaeopteryx* fell into the water, drowned, and sank almost undisturbed to the bottom. The fossils include bones, beak, teeth, claws, and the all-important feathers – with even their delicate shafts and veins visible – which identify these animals as birds beyond any doubt.

3. Extra feathers fall from a preening *Archaeopteryx*. The feather is the key feature that separates birds from all other animals. It is made of keratin, the same protein that forms the outer skin, scales,

and claws of reptiles (and the outer skin, claws, nails, horns, and hooves of mammals). Only six sets of *Archaeopteryx* fossils have been found, and one of these is a single feather. The feather's proportions are similar to a modern bird's flight feathers, indicating that *Archaeopteryx* could really fly.

4. One bird's wing bars are a different color. Female and male *Archaeopteryx* may have been distinguished in this way, just like many of today's bird species. However, there are no real clues to the color of *Archaeopteryx*'s feathers.

5. Teeth disappear from *Archaeopteryx*'s beak. The first-known bird was a curious mix of reptile and bird features. It was still evolving from its reptilian ancestor – a small, two-legged dinosaur resembling *Compsognathus* (see page 16). *Archaeopteryx* retained sharp reptilian teeth in its bird-like beak. Later birds lost the heavy teeth but kept the lightweight beak; as their weight dropped, they became better fliers.

6. Claws appear, grasping the tree bark. The arm of *Archaeopteryx* was still evolving into a wing. It already had long upper-arm and forearm bones, like later birds, but it also retained three long, clawed reptile-like fingers. These fingers were ideal for gripping and climbing on bark and tree limbs.

7. *Archaeopteryx* has lost its toe at the back. The earliest-known bird had its first toe facing backward, and the other three pointing forward (the fifth had disappeared). Most birds of today have this same foot plan. It is ideal for hooking around a narrow twig, or for digging into the bark of a larger branch.

8. An *Archaeopteryx* has a tail made solely of long feathers. *Archaeopteryx* had a feathered tail, to help steer and balance as it ran and flew, but the middle of its tail was formed by a chain of vertebrae extending from the hips – another sign of its reptilian ancestry. Modern birds have lost their bony tails entirely and now have only a short, small stump of bones called the pygostyle, which is hardly visible on the outside. Their tails are composed only of feathers.

9. Another *Archaeopteryx* has joined a V formation. *Archaeopteryx* was a chicken-size bird, about 2 feet (60 centimeters) from the tip of its beak to the tip of its tail. Its wingspan was probably about the same length. The shapes of the fossilized arm and breast bones show that *Archaeopteryx* lacked the large, powerful chest muscles that flap the wings of today's birds. Its flight was probably weak and clumsy, fluttering down from trees after climbing into them with its hand and foot claws. Therefore this V formation, used by long-distance fliers such as geese, was a very unlikely scenario.

10. A small dinosaur flaps its arms while running after food. There are many theories about why birds took to the air. They may have pursued flying insects and evolved arm feathers to help them leap higher into the air. Perhaps the feathers evolved to help them swoop down from trees to the ground. Or the feathers were mostly a "net" for catching prey, only later developing into flying apparatus. Or they evolved for insulation and protection. Or…

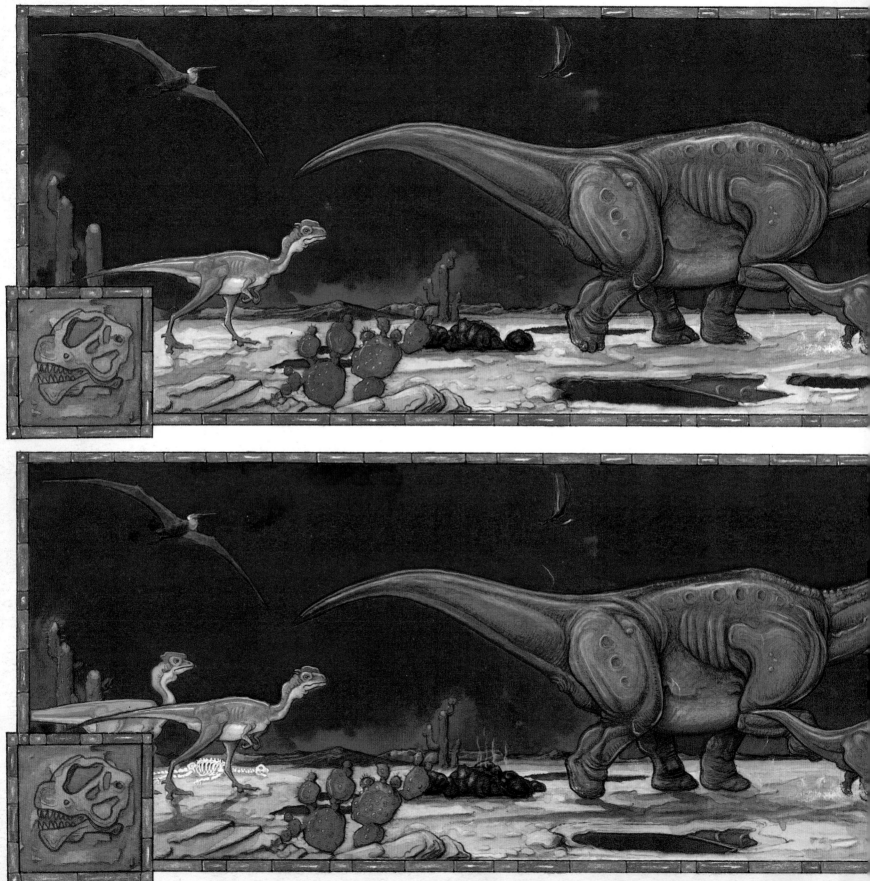

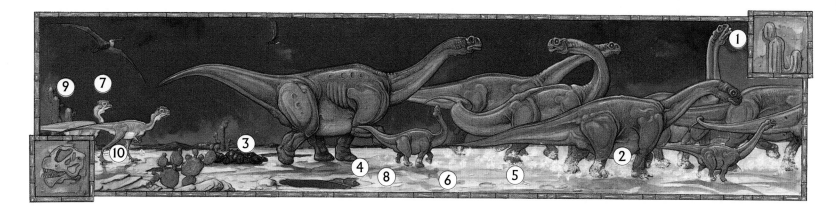

TIME: A combined scene from the Early Jurassic Period, 200 million years ago, and the Late Jurassic Period, 150 million years ago

PLACE: Western North America

DINOSAURS: *Dilophosaurus*, a medium-size Early Jurassic theropod; *Camarasaurus*, a huge Late Jurassic sauropod

Giants in the Desert

The seasonal rains are still several weeks away. The landscape is parched and dry. The herd of *Camarasaurus* has grazed until the only remaining greenery is too prickly to eat. It's time to move on. The 20-ton sauropods stride out powerfully across the desert, their barrel bodies carried on long elephant-like legs. As they travel, their large, high-set nostrils sniff the wind for the scent of vegetation. But instead, the wind brings the smell of danger: *Dilophosaurus* trails the herd, waiting for the chance to attack a straggler.

1. *Camarasaurus* **is eating a pebble.** A pebble? Compared to many of its sauropod relatives, *Camarasaurus* had strong jaws and jaw muscles, and sizable teeth shaped like sharpened spoons. These teeth were ideal for snipping and shearing through tough vegetation, even twigs and bark. However, they were not suitable for chewing; the dinosaur gulped down its food whole and also swallowed pebbles or stones. The stones and food were ground together by contractions (squeezing movements) of the animal's thick, muscular gizzard. This action – a substitute for chewing – crushed the plant material and kick-started digestion. The stones – called gizzard stones or gastroliths – became ultra-smooth in the process, and this is how we find them today, still associated with the belly area of certain fossil skeletons.

2. *Camarasaurus* **is fatter.** The dinosaur's belly has been swollen by gases from digesting plant material. It had bathtub-size gut chambers to digest the huge quantities of food it ate. This process extracted the maximum amount of nutrients from its diet.

3. The herd leaves more evidence of its passing, in the form of droppings. Large quantities of fossilized "dino dung" have been discovered. Of course, it is no longer smelly. It is preserved as pieces of solid rock, known as coprolites. The shape and size of the coprolites, and their fossil contents such as seeds or twigs, indicate the dinosaur's diet.

4. *Camarasaurus* **loses its "toenails."** The toenails were actually small, stubby claws. The front inner claw (the "thumb") was longer and curved, and may have been used for self-defense. Like its cousins *Brachiosaurus* and *Diplodocus*, the 60-foot (18-meter) *Camarasaurus* stood on tiptoes. The enormous body weight was spread out much like a modern elephant's, via a broad, flat sole the size of a pillowcase. This weight distribution worked so well that if you and *Camarasaurus* walked across the same soft mud, your footprints would be deeper.

5. More footprints appear in the soft sand. Scientists believe that sauropods traveled in herds because they have found many fossilized sauropod footprints, or trackways, together. These trackways were probably made by a group.

6. The shadows are different because the sun's position has changed. How did *Camarasaurus* find fresh pastures? It may have lumbered aimlessly in search of food, rather than travel a regular, seasonal migration. But an awareness of the sun's position through the day would have helped the dinosaurs travel in a useful straight line, instead of in a useless circle.

7. A second *Dilophosaurus* joins its colleague. These lithe, long-tailed hunters were among the earliest large theropods – the group of two-legged meat-eating dinosaurs that included *Allosaurus* and *Tyrannosaurus*. The curious head crest consisted of two roughly semicircular ridges of bone, set on edge in the top of the skull, forming a V shape when viewed from the front.

Hence the dinosaur's name, which means "two-ridge reptile." *Dilophosaurus* was around 20 feet (6 meters) long, stood 8 feet (2.5 meters) tall, and represented half a ton of speedy, sharp-fanged predator.

8. The puddle has dried out in the sun. In general, the Jurassic climate was warm and moist. But in the interiors of the great landmasses, some deserts remained. The little water that fell as rain, or condensed as dew, was soon burned away by the fierce sun.

9. The desert plants sprout more prickly stems. True cacti, being flowering plants, had probably not yet evolved (see page 37). However, some plants, such as certain cycads, had fat stems for storing moisture, and spines and prickles for defense against hungry herbivores.

10. The desert has claimed another victim. Thirst was the primary killer in such dry countryside. But death fueled life. Insects and other small animals lapped up the blood and body fluids of the carcass, and scavenging creatures picked at the flesh and gristle. Eventually the remains rotted back into the soil, and, when the rains finally arrived, plants sprang up from the enriched earth.

TIME: A combined scene from the Late Jurassic Period, 150 million years ago, and the Late Cretaceous Period, 70 million years ago

PLACE: Midwestern North America

DINOSAURS: *Stegosaurus*, a four-legged Jurassic plant-eater with large upright plates along its back; *Parasaurolophus*, one of the Cretaceous crested hadrosaurs ("duck-bills") with a long, tubular skull projection

C r e s t s   f o r C o u r t s h i p

It's that time again! During the breeding season each species of dinosaur gets together with others of its kind to mate. Some reptiles today, especially lizards and snakes, have elaborate courtship rituals in which they flash and wave brightly colored parts of their bodies, take a set pattern of body positions, and go through specific actions. They hiss and make other sounds and emit sexual scents. Did dinosaurs do the same? Quite possibly. Some dinosaurs had large plates or crests projecting from their bodies. These might have been brightly colored visual signals, for saying to a potential partner: "Choose me! I'm fit and healthy and will be a fine mate!"

1. The tubular crests of *Parasaurolophus* are a different color. *Parasaurolophus* was one of several hadrosaurs that possessed a large bony crest on the skull. The crest shapes differed from one type of hadrosaur to another, and perhaps served to distinguish the various species in large mixed herds. In this re-creation, female *Parasaurolophus* are distinguished from males by the shape of their crests rather than by their color. Males had a tubular crest about 3 feet (1 meter) long. The female's crest is only half this length and more curved.

2. *Parasaurolophus* blows out its breath and flares its nostrils. It is calling for a mate, with low trumpeting sounds. The breathing passages ran from the nostrils, along the upper inside of the tubular crest to its tip, and then looped back along the lower part of the crest, and down into the neck and windpipe. The dinosaur breathed or blew in a certain way to make the hollow crest vibrate and so make its love song louder. Because the males had crests that were twice as long as those of the females, their sounds would have been much deeper.

3. **The eggs of *Parasaurolophus* are colored for camouflage.** This hadrosaur was a fairly close relative of another "duck-bill," *Maiasaura* (see page 40), and may have built its nests in the same way. Dull, mottled shells would help the eggs to blend in with their surroundings and make them less likely to be noticed by predators. When the baby dinosaurs hatched, they were probably about a foot (30 centimeters) long. The adult *Parasaurolophus* grew to 32 feet (10 meters) in length and stood more than 10 feet (3 meters) high.

4. ***Stegosaurus* is missing one of its back plates.** The flattened, diamond-shaped plates of bone, with their lower edges embedded in the skin along the back, were probably in two upright rows, one set slightly farther back behind the other. What were these extraordinary structures for? Well...

5. **The back plates of *Stegosaurus* are a different color on the inner surface.** One explanation for the plates is that they helped the dinosaur to control its body temperature. In hot conditions, the plates worked like radiators, pumping excess body warmth into the air. When it was cool, the plates acted like heat absorbers, soaking up the sun's warmth. The heat was distributed around the dinosaur's body by its blood, which flowed through plentiful vessels sandwiched between the skin surface and bony core of each plate.

6. ***Stegosaurus* is moving – in a slow courtship dance.** A second suggestion for the stegosaur's back plates is that they were used for communication. Possibly the skin on the plates was colorfully patterned, providing a striking visual display as *Stegosaurus* swayed to and fro moving its head from side to side. Perhaps different sexes had different patterns or the color of the plates changed during the mating season.

7. ***Stegosaurus'* eye is open.** All the suggestions that have been made about visual signals would make sense only if dinosaurs had reasonable eyesight and were able to see in color. The orbits (eye sockets) in their fossilized skulls indicate that dinosaur eyes were similar to those of modern reptiles. So it's likely that dinosaurs could see well – especially moving objects. However, it is all guesswork. You'd have to be a dinosaur to know how dinosaurs saw!

8. **The tail spikes of *Stegosaurus* are more upright.** The probable position for the four tail spikes was midway between vertical and horizontal. These long, sharp, bony-centered parts were almost certainly used for defense. *Stegosaurus* would swing them at attackers like a multi-spiked club.

9. ***Stegosaurus* moves its front leg forward.** This 3-ton, 26-foot (8-meter) dinosaur had four longish legs, and walked with its body well off the ground. Its brain was no larger than a walnut, and scientists once thought that, to help control its massive bulk, there would need to be a second "brain" in its tail. Preserved bones show that there were bulges in the main nerve cords in *Stegosaurus'* hips, but these were probably nerve relay stations, and not a second brain.

10. **The sun is nearly below the horizon.** In the heat of midday, the dinosaurs would have rested in the cool shade. As the sun descended and evening drew near, these great beasts would have been at their most active, feeding and courting and calling.

TIME: The Middle Cretaceous Period, 100 million years ago

PLACE: Western North America

REPTILES: *Deinonychus*, a swift and powerful two-legged predator of the dromaeosaur group; *Centrosaurus*, a ceratopsian ("horned dinosaur")

Ambush on the Plains

While crossing a dry, rocky plain, a small group of *Centrosaurus* are being ambushed by a hunting pack of the fierce dromaeosaurs known as *Deinonychus*. The horned dinosaurs were on their way to another lowland area to munch on leaves and stems. Although the *Centrosaurus* are far larger and heavier than their attackers and form themselves into a defensive huddle, the dromaeosaurs are fast, powerful, and agile. They work as a team, attacking from all sides. Soon one of the horned dinosaurs will be injured beyond recovery and fall prey to the dromaeosaurs, while the others lumber to safety.

1. *Deinonychus* attacks with its slashing claw. This dromaeosaur's name means "terrible claw." Its main attacking weapon – a large, sharp, curving claw – was on the second toe of each foot. Special joints and muscles linked the claw to the foot. *Deinonychus* normally held the claw up and back, away from the ground, to keep it sharp. But in a flash it could kick its leg and stick out its claw, slashing with tremendous speed and power.

2. *Centrosaurus* bleeds from a wound. The front end of this 3-ton herbivore was well protected by the frontal horn and the bony, frilled shield over its face and neck. But the ambushers attacked from the rear, too. Their slashing claws left gaping gashes in the flanks of this *Centrosaurus*.

3. *Deinonychus* is hurled around. The battle was not one-sided. As the *Centrosaurus* members faced outward, trying to protect each other's rear ends, one grabbed the tail of a *Deinonychus* in its mouth. The predator was swung around like a rag doll. The sharp, beak-like front of the ceratopsian's mouth bit so deep into

the tail of the predator that the tail end was cut from its owner. The gathering pterosaurs in the sky above will just as happily eat a dead *Deinonychus* as the remains of a *Centrosaurus*.

4. *Centrosaurus* has broken its horn. The long nose-horn was this lumbering herbivore's main defensive weapon. The nose-horn had a core of bone and was covered by a sharp-tipped sheath of horny material. The dinosaur would lower its head, charge, and jab upward, like the modern-day rhinoceros. It also had two much smaller horns on the brows of its eyes.

5. A young *Centrosaurus* hides among the adults. The large adults may have formed a defensive circle to enclose and protect the smaller, weaker members of their group. The array of horns and neck shields would present a formidable barrier. Modern large herbivores such as musk ox and yak take up the same formation against pack predators like wolves.

6. A huge skull has appeared in the background. The *Deinonychus* pack has hunted here before. This is the remains of their previous kill. For their body size, these dinosaurs had relatively large brains. Perhaps they remembered the ambush site from last time. Open, rocky country would be ideal for their stalk-and-pounce technique, since they were long-limbed and could run much faster than the pillar-legged ceratopsians. (Fossils of *Deinonychus* date from several million years before those of *Centrosaurus*. But the encounter depicted here happened many times between dromaeosaurs and ceratopsians of various kinds.)

7. More pterosaurs appear in the sky. Some of these winged reptiles may have filled the ecological niche (role) that vultures and condors occupy today. They would soar and wheel at great height, using thermals (currents of warm, rising air) to save energy, and watching with their large eyes for the rich pickings of a large carcass. Once the *Deinonychus* group had moved on, they would flap in to feast.

8. A small salamander appears on a rock. Salamanders are amphibians, tailed relatives of frogs and toads. They first appeared during the Late Jurassic Period. Although outwardly lizard-like, they have moist skin and need damp conditions to survive. This plains salamander spent most of its day in a cool burrow under the rocks. It emerged at night to hunt insects and other small creatures and soak up the dew.

9. A desert plant comes into bloom. The Cretaceous Period saw the appearance of flowering plants, or angiosperms. With almost explosive speed, they spread across the land, evolving into many different types. On the plains, and along the shores of rivers and lakes, they began to replace the conifers and other earlier plants.

10. The rocks are getting higher! The Cretaceous Period saw a great era of mountain-building around the world, as the earth's enormous continental blocks drifted and collided with each other. Their edges became buckled and bent into the ripples we call mountains. The Rocky Mountains in North America, the site of our plains ambush, date from Middle to Late Cretaceous times.

TIME: The Late Cretaceous Period, 70 million years ago
PLACE: Midwestern North America (now Montana)
REPTILES: *Maiasaura*, a medium-size hadrosaur;
Troodon, a small meat-eater; *Pteranodon*, one of the
largest and most agile of the pterosaurs; *Oviraptor*, a
small dinosaur that robbed the nests of other dinosaurs.

A Place to Nest

Thousands of *Maiasaura* have
migrated across the flat, coastal
plains of Late Cretaceous North
America. Now they arrive at their
traditional nesting sites, in an
open area of loose, muddy soil where
approaching enemies are easily spotted. For
dinosaurs, as for animals in breeding colonies
today, mating and rearing young is a time of
danger. As the babies develop and hatch from
their eggs, there is danger from the stomping
feet of their parents and neighbors. Small
predatory dinosaurs might sneak among the
nests, under cover of darkness, and steal the
eggs or the hatchlings. And there are always
bigger predators skirting the colony, ready to
pick off an unwary adult.

1. The *Maiasaura* scoops up more earth around her nest.
An amazing series of fossil finds in Montana revealed the remains
of hundreds of the 30-foot (9-meter) long hadrosaurs *Maiasaura*
("good mother reptile"), as well as dinosaur nests, eggs,
hatchlings, and older youngsters. The fossils show shallow nest
holes, scooped out by pushing the mud to make a raised rim about
6 1/2 feet (2 meters) in diameter.

2. The *Maiasaura* moves her head threateningly, ready to
defend her nest site. *Maiasaura* nests were regularly spaced
across the colony. Each one was, in fact, just beyond biting
distance of its neighbors – the same way today's seabirds space
their nests. A nest site was a valuable piece of real estate,
especially toward the middle of the colony, where the risk of attack
from marauding predators was lowest.

3. Cracks appear in the egg. It's ready to hatch. Fossil fragments
suggest that 20 or so oval eggs, each 6 inches (20 centimeters)
long, were laid in the muddy scoop and then covered with a layer

of rotting vegetation. The warmth from this compost-heap incubator helped the babies to develop, and the covering hid the eggs. When the eggs were about to hatch, the mother *Maiasaura* probably raked away the plants.

4. An eggshell lies broken on the sand. The young *Maiasaura* has broken out of its shelly container, to begin life in the open. Perhaps it used an "egg tooth," a sharp tooth-like growth on the end of its snout, to slit and crack the shell. Some fossil shell fragments have been crushed, perhaps by the feet of older youngsters, who may have also lived in the nest.

5. A newly-hatched *Maiasaura* will not survive because it has been born with misshapen legs. In any animal species, there are always babies who begin with a disadvantage. They may be born too early, or very weak, or not properly formed. For these babies, life is short. Sad it may be, but it's a fact of nature. Only individuals who are healthy and best suited to the environment tend to survive. This keeps the whole species thriving and successful.

6. A mother *Maiasaura* brings food to her nestful of babies. The many fossils of *Maiasaura* excavated (dug up) since the late 1970s revolutionized our ideas about dinosaur reproduction. The newly-hatched babies did not have legs that were strong enough to carry them around. They stayed in the nest for the first few weeks of their lives. Yet their preserved teeth show signs of wear, suggesting they ate food. Perhaps the mother brought plants back to the nest for them.

7. An older *Maiasaura* is still with its mother. In addition to the preserved remains of hatchlings about 10 inches (30 centimeters) long, the Montana fossils also contain the bones of bigger, older youngsters, over 3 feet (1 meter) long. Did the offspring stay with their parent, for months or even years? Did they live as a family? Or were they just loose groups, coming and going at random?

8. An egg-thieving *Troodon* is startled into dropping its prize. This small predator had slim limbs and a large head with big eyes. Although it was almost 7 feet (2 meters) long, it would stand only waist-high to a human. *Troodon* fossils were found with those of *Maiasaura*, suggesting that this alert, agile predator sneaked among the nests, looking for unguarded eggs and babies. Here, the far larger *Maiasaura* threatens *Troodon* into releasing the egg. However, *Oviraptor*, taking advantage of the confusion, sneaks in to steal an egg undetected.

9. As dusk approaches, the moon emerges. With its large eyes, *Troodon* would be well equipped to see and grab prey during the gloom of dawn and dusk. Twilight was therefore a risky time for the animals *Troodon* preyed on, and *Maiasaura* had to be alert to the sounds and scents around it, and to the vibrations of footsteps carried through the ground.

10. A *Pteranodon* returns to its roost with a fish dinner. The winged reptiles, called pterosaurs, were once thought to be heavy, ungainly gliders. Now opinions have changed, and they are seen as aerobatic, strongly flapping soarers. These pterosaurs were *Pteranodon*, a large species with a wingspan of up to 30 feet (9 meters). They soared over the shallow seas by day, swooping down to grab fish in their long, toothless "beaks."

TIME: The Late Cretaceous Period, 65 million years ago

PLACE: Northwestern North America (now Alberta, Canada)

DINOSAURS: *Tyrannosaurus*, the largest predatory dinosaur; *Triceratops*, one of the horned plant-eaters known as ceratopsians; also birds and mammals of the time

A Catastrophe

The huge and fierce hunter *Tyrannosaurus* charges from the edge of a forest, as one of its potential victims, a *Triceratops*, lies sick and dying nearby. If you could visit this same landscape one million years later, you would spot a much greater change than the differences shown here. No dinosaurs at all! About 65 million years ago, a mysterious worldwide catastrophe, or disaster, wiped out all of the dinosaurs. It also killed off all of the flying pterosaurs, most sea reptiles such as ichthyosaurs and mosasaurs, and numerous other groups of animals. Lots of plants vanished, too. The differences between these two scenes hint at possible causes of the catastrophic mass extinction that brought the Age of the Dinosaurs to an end and began the Age of the Mammals.

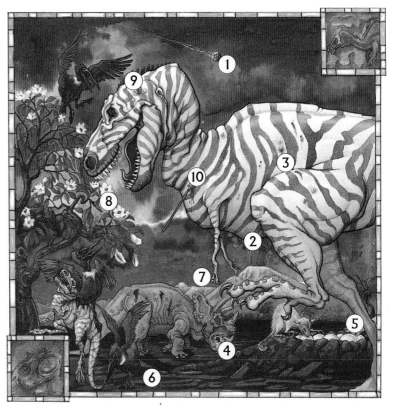

1. **The meteor grows larger in the sky.** One of the favorite explanations for the catastrophe is that a meteorite hit the planet. A gigantic lump of rock, over 6 miles (10 kilometers) across, bigger than the comet fragments that smashed into Jupiter in 1994, could have hurtled from outer space and smashed into the Earth – possibly at a site that is now under the sea off southeast Mexico. The resulting explosion could have thrown up massive clouds of ash and dust that encircled the Earth and blotted out the sun. Animals used to high temperatures would have been unable to survive the resulting cold, and plants would have died in the cool gloom, having a devastating effect on the food chains and animal life. However, the dinosaurs didn't disappear suddenly but gradually over a million years or more.

2. **The volcano erupts and spews out lava and smoke.** Another possible cause of the mass extinction was a series of massive volcanic eruptions around the globe which belched ash clouds and poisonous fumes into the atmosphere. Animals died in the choking gases. However, this idea has the same flaw as most of the others. Why did only certain animals, like the dinosaurs and the pterosaurs, die,

while similar groups, such as the crocodiles and turtles, survived? So far, there is no answer to this puzzle.

3. *Tyrannosaurus* is covered with skin sores and ulcers. Yuck! Perhaps an outbreak of sunspots or some other cosmic event showered the Earth with harmful radiation. This would have caused skin cancers, blindness, and other terrible diseases among susceptible animals. (Think about the ozone hole today – a perilous parallel?)

4. *Triceratops* foams at the mouth. Why? Because it had eaten plants that had evolved poisonous chemicals as a defense. The Cretaceous Period saw the rise of flowering plants, possibly with new methods of self-defense against herbivores such as the 30-foot (9-meter), 5-ton *Triceratops*.

5. Another small mammal appears, to sniff the dinosaur eggs hungrily. Mammals had been around almost as long as the dinosaurs, but they were small and insignificant. If the meteorite theory is correct, the dinosaurs' metabolism may have slowed down in the cool conditions, making them unable to protect their eggs. Warm-blooded mammals such as *Alphadon* would have been able to scamper about just as quickly as before and steal the eggs.

6. The bird has webbed feet. This is *Ichthyornis*, a bird with tiny teeth and strong flapping wings. Its webbed feet indicate it was a shorebird. As well as eating fish, it probably preyed on eggs and baby dinosaurs, and competed with juvenile dinosaurs for small-animal prey. Was the dinosaurs' food source diminished by rising new groups such as birds and mammals?

7. *Tyrannosaurus* has a different number of fingers. *Tyrannosaurus'* two-fingered arms were so small that they could not reach up to put food into its mouth. Some experts contend that this massive 6-ton predator could charge its prey at speeds of more than 20 mph (32 km/h), bringing down its victims with its teeth after a short chase. Others believe it was simply a lumbering scavenger.

8. Flowers have opened on the magnolia tree. The speedy spread and beautiful blossoming of flowering plants must have greatly altered the balance of nature in a relatively short time. The dinosaurs first appeared in a very different world, 160 million years previously. Perhaps they were unsuited to eating or digesting the newer types of vegetation.

9. *Tyrannosaurus* has a spiked crest on its head. This may have been true. If the crest was made only of skin, it would be unlikely to fossilize. We must always remember that fossil records represent a very selective preservation. There are many gaps in the story of evolution.

10. A spear pierces the *Tyrannosaurus*. This final difference is something of a joke. In certain dinosaur movies and books, we see people using spears and clubs to hunt dinosaurs. The dinosaurs then get their revenge by tearing the people to pieces. In fact, the last dinosaurs and the first humans were separated by at least 60 million years. The "terrible reptiles" were all gone by around 65 million years ago. The first humans appeared on Earth less than three million years ago.